Doorman

Geoff Thompson

SUMMERSDALE

Summersdale Publishers Ltd
46 West Street
Chichester
West Sussex
PO19 1RP
England

www.summersdale.com

ISBN 1 84024 373 2

Printed and bound in Great Britain by Biddles Ltd.

Note:
This play may not be performed without written permission
from the publisher. Please write to the above address if you
would like to discuss obtaining a licence to perform it.

Special thanks to:
All at the Royal Court Theatre, London, for taking me into
their writers' group and for guiding me with this play.
Especially to the very gracious Ian Rickson, Graham
Whybrow and Dominic Cooke.

Lil Warren whose tenacity and writing talent inspired the
writing of this play.

John Lennegan for kindly reading the first draft and offering
much-appreciated feedback.

Martin Carr for his undying support, love and friendship and
for his faith in me and my writing.

Jim Cartwright for his inspiration and for spending a day
with me reading Draft One of this play.

Michael Vale and Paul Crewes for taking a chance on me and
for their patience, faith and very welcome friendship.

Victor Gardener for having the bollocks to be the first to play
Tony.

The Drum Theatre Plymouth
In association with Crewes Gale Productions Ltd Present

DOORMAN

By Geoff Thompson

Produced by Paul Crewes

Directed & Designed by Michael Vale

Lighting designed by Tim Skelly

Music composed by Phelan Kane & Steve Hopwood

Performed by Victor Gardener

Casting by Kay Magson

29 January – 08 February 2003

In the stage play, *Doorman*, Tony has to break free from a cycle of violence that is changing him into a man he no longer recognises and does not want to be. But has he left it too late?

Writer **Geoff Thompson** was himself 'on the door' for nine years at some of the toughest nightclubs in the UK. Since then he has published over twenty books, including his autobiographical bestseller *Watch My Back*. His multi-award-nominated short screenplay *Bouncer*, starring Ray Winstone, was premiered at the Edinburgh Festival in 2002.

Doorman is his first stage play.

Foreword

I will never underestimate anything ever again.

I have always believed that it is in us all to achieve anything we set our intentions on. I believe that there is nothing beyond our capacity; we are a species born to create. Whilst this is true, and I believe it with all my heart, I have to admit that in approaching this play I was one of those arrogant people that would watch the staging of a play and think, or even say (oh the embarrassment); 'That looks easy enough. I could do that.'

It was after such a statement that I sat down to write *Doorman*, or *One Sock* as it was originally called. Three years later (I naively thought it might take a few weeks to write, find a producer, director, actor, rehearsal rooms, theatre, money, money and more money and the bottle before the staging and subsequent – imagined – critical acclaim!) I have arrived at the Drum Theatre Plymouth, my arrogance already decapitated and placed on a deterrent-spike, keenly aware that other haughty, would-be playwrights will be watching and thinking/ saying the same thing.

I have learned much in the three years that it has taken to get this baby together, not least that nothing is simple, even (and perhaps especially) if it looks as if it is. I have also realised that collaboration means much more than I originally thought. Without the help of so many people – The Royal Court, London, my friend Martin Carr, producer Paul Crewes and Director Michael Vale specifically – this thing would probably have never left the Doc 1 file on my computer. It is a very humbling experience to see just how much work goes into taking a play from page to stage. I was staggered and impressed. I was also very impatient. So for my arrogance, for my ignorance and for my impatience (all three are on my 'must improve' list) I would like to apologise. Sorry.

This is my first play, hopefully the first of many. I am going to try my hand at a four man (or woman) play next. I watched one the other day and, between you and me I reckon I could do it, it looked easy enough...

Geoff Thompson

Doorman

A bare stage, not necessarily black. Double EXIT doors, a table, a chair and a short bench.

We hear the dull monotonous boom-boom of nightclub music from somewhere deep behind the doors. Suddenly, and without warning, they explode violently open. Immediately the dull boom-boom of the music hits the stage at full volume. It is loud and frenzied. Flashing disco lights from inside the club light up the stage. Plumes of dry ice and cigarette smoke pour from the EXIT doors.

*A bouncer (**Tony**) violently hauls an imaginary customer backwards, in a headlock, from the club. The struggle is violent and ugly.*

He slams his victim onto the floor and stamps on him many times, almost in rhythm with the background music and flashing lights. The slaughter is frenzied and uncomfortable to watch. The bouncer's face contorts into a mask of hate, plate-sized gobs of spit flick from his mouth.

The stamping ends.

Doorman

The doorman is seething under his breath, his chest heaving.
Very slowly he circles his imaginary foe. Suddenly and violently
he kicks him once more, letting out a fearsome scream, then
holds his own ankle and grimaces in pain as though the kick
has hurt his foot.

He takes a handkerchief out of his top pocket, bends over and
wipes the blood from his polished shoe.

The music pouring from the club is uncomfortable. **Tony**
glances at the open EXIT doors, moves across and closes them,
relegating the sound to its original dull boom.

Tony *fidgets with his right sock.*

Tony: Fuckin' racket! Cabbages me. Shit like that fucks
with your brain. It's got to do, innit? Sometimes it takes
me days to get that Boom fuckin' Boom out of me
swede. I lie in bed at night and all I can hear is Boom
Boom fuckin' Boom. On an' on. Cabbages me.

He wipes blood from his sock.

Fuck, I 'ate it when it gets on me sock. I 'ate the mess. I
'ate the wet of someone else's blood being sucked
through the cotton and into me skin. It's like he's still a

threat. And it's not just blood – piss, too. Piss! I'm not jestin'. These fuckers will attack you with anythin', even their bodily fluids.

Threw a Doris out one night for bein' ugly and frightenin' the other customers – gruesome thing, face on it like a Scotch egg. Throws 'er out – physical like 'cos she refused to leave – she's hit the deck hard, like she's fell off a block of flats, and the boyfriend's ran at me like a demented thing. I'm just about to land a heavy right when bang! He pulls out 'is dick and pisses up me ankles. Puddles in me turn-ups, steam rising from me socks, disgustin'. Straight up, pissed on me. 'S fuckin' embarrassin'. I was fumin'. Before I had a chance to retaliate he's zipped up and fucked off. Gone. Never to be seen again. The other lads were gagging themselves, rolling around the floor like hyenas. Piss? I stunk for days.

This one guy I chinned was sick everywhere. It was in his hair, in his coat, fucking right mess. Never whack anyone after they've just 'ad a Ruby Murray and a Guinness six-pack – let me tell ya, it's a dry cleaner's nightmare. Blood and puke and snot and his head layin' on it like on a pillow. See, I was fairly new to it then. I felt dead sorry for him. Killer Kenny cracked up. He goes, 'All the colour's ran out of your arse'ole, Tony, you've gone all pale at the gills.' It was the hollow thud when his head hit the pavement, and that 'orrible gargle as he gagged on his own blood. Bluaarr! Kenny just walked over, colder than a snowman's gonads, flicked his fag into the sick and said, 'Fat bastard.'

He's a man of few words. Speaks like he's being charged by the letter. He doesn't need words, he's got his own language, a kind of physicality that transcends the need for speak. His way of telling you that he likes you is putting you in a headlock. Nice. How the fuck his missus manages I'll never know. While other girls are getting flowers and chocolates she's getting the intricacies of a carotid strangle and a sleeper. Can you imagine the sex? Foreplay must be like a muggin'. Kenny. Killer we call him, because he is. Clint Eastwood in a dinner jacket. A master of violence. A right hook like a fucking piston. It only moves about this far – (*shows*) – about six inches, that's all he needs and BANG! They're off the planet, out of the game before they even know they're in it. Scary. He frightens the brown stuff out of me and I know 'im.

I remember this one situation, it was a beauty, a peach, some penis was givin' me a bit of that – (*shows nagging*

Doorman

with hand) – tryin' to get large, so I slaps him, wallop! (*Shows*) Nothin'! He doesn't even flinch, it was like hitting the side of a house. 'Is that it?' he goes, 'Is that your best shot? My sister could 'it harder than that.' Bang! Before he could say another word Kenny's hit him with a left hook that might have been shot from a cannon and the lad's out of there. No pre-amble, no 'ow's your father, just bang! He's out of there. Kenny looks down at this twitching mound of unconsciousness, 'Can she hit harder than that?'

It don't matter who you are or what you've got. If he lands that left you're kippin'. Even had one of them martial arts types try it on with him one night. Stood there giving it that – (*shows some exaggerated kung fu poses*) – Ohhhaaaa! Hayai! Kenny goes to me, 'I think we've got us a karate man, Tony.' One left hook later and the lad's asleep with his teeth lying on the pavement next to him in a pool of blood. 'My mistake, Tony,' he says, 'He was a kung fu man.'

It was a copper who summed him up. He goes, 'Kenny's got a very short vocabulary and when he runs out of words he hits anything with a pulse'. We had to move an off-duty copper one night. We found him in the toilet swimmin' in regurgitated chicken korma.

Doorman

Actually, it didn't look much different to when they serve it at the curry house with a pint of lager and a poppadom. There's never a rush to eject a punter with a jacket full of sick, I can tell you. It's one of them jobs. Handling people who leave what's left of last night's dinner on the toilet floor. They're a nightmare, night-fuckin'-mare. It's us that have to get them out, you know.

I looked at Horlicks – we called him that 'cos he's always putting people to sleep last thing at night – I said, 'What is it with me and people shouting Hughie?' I reckon I must be a sick magnet, I seem to attract them all. It's a worry, I have to say. Anyway, between us we got the lad out – funny lookin' fucker, thin tash that barely covered the hair-lip-cleft-palate scenario. We carried him out like that – (*shows*) – trying our hardest not to get any lumps on the cloth. Tricky when you consider the fact that the lad is flailin' about like an epi. Got him outside, relatively unsoiled, and closed the door. Job done. Or so we thought. Within seconds he's banging on the door with all the authority of an off-duty-pissed-up-sicked-over-probably-still-on-probation police constable. Horlicks opens the door.

'What?'

Doorman

'I want to come back in.'

Like he's actually in with a chance. 'I'm all right now,' and he's brushing diced and curried carrot off his tweed as he says it. Horlicks, not one to mince his words – told a judge once, a Doris who'd just given him eighteen months for ABH, that he hoped her next baby was a hedgehog – he goes to the hair-lip, 'Fuck off – you smell!' Not gonna win diplomat of the year, I grant you, but at least the lad knew where he stood.

That's when he produces his police ID card, thrusts it out like that – (*shows*) – as though we're gonna drag out the red carpet and give him a free tab at the bar. Horlicks takes a good look. 'Hold on one mo,' he says as he disappears back into the club. Seconds later he peeps his head back around the door. 'Let's have another look at that ID again.' So the lad thrusts the card in front of him, and he's wearin' this smug grin like we're bang to rights, like he's won. Whoosh! Horlicks lets rip with a fire extinguisher and drenches the poor fucker, drenches him, he's soaked to the skin. 'I told you once, fuck off!' Well, I was crying, my ribs were hurting I laughed so much. Me and Horlicks rollin' around the floor in bits and all we can hear outside is this drippy voice shouting, 'That's not funny.'

Doorman

That's not funny. Brilliant.

Tell you what was funny though – well I say funny, it was more weird than it was funny. I sparked this one guy who'd squared up for the straight'ner and his fuckin' shoe flew off. Honest. I hit him and it just flew off. Not the left one, just the right. I've never seen anythin' like it in my life. Unprecedented. He went one way and his fuckin' shoe went the other. Strange. It was like it was abandoning ship. Deserting the ranks. I had visions of this fuckin' shoe divin' out of the fracas screamin', 'I'm a soft Italian brogue, I don't do violence.' Fuckin' comin' to summat when you can't even rely on yer shoes in a crisis.

An' listen to this fucker; when 'e's out 'e's thrown up and just for the crack someone banged the shoe right in the middle of the sick, a black polished brogue floating in puke. When he woke up, that was the first thing he saw. 'Fuckin' hell, I don't remember eating that.' Fuckin' brilliant! Sterlin'. Can you imagine it?

And get this, listen, the paramedic came – 'cos the guy was in a bad way, fuckin' looked like he'd been machine gunned – he turns up, takes one look at the mess and

Doorman

goes, 'I bet he drinks Carling Black Label.' Brilliant. I chinned another guy – listen, listen – sparked him with a right, his head smashed off a wall, then off a door edge and cracked like an egg on the pavement, 'is swede was like a fuckin' pinball; ding, ding, ding. (*Laughs*) Shouldn't laugh but I can't help meself. As his head bounced off all these inanimate objects, we was all going, 'Ohh, ohh, ohh,' as though it was our heads. Fuckin' hurt just to watch. (*Looks at his right fist*) Mind you, I like me right, got a homing device on it. Once I let this baby go it does the job all on its own. It's a good job too 'cos most nights it's like fuckin' Beirut in here.

We get some right head-the-balls. We 'ave to search 'em for blades, craft knives, carpet cutters, samurai swords – a guy pulled a fuckin' pair of garden shears on me one night, no duff, fucking grass cutters! Spaceman. Kenny always says, 'You 'ave to stop the shit at the door. Once it gets inside you might as well stick your 'ead between your legs and kiss your bollocks goodbye. 'Ere's a for-instance. I remember when Kenny did old Twenty Neck, a big fuck off rugger player with a neck like that – (*shows*) – face like ten boxers, cauliflowers for ears, digger-bucket hands, a model for wanted posters, you know the type. Horrible as bastards.

Doorman

Anyway, he did the park with Kenny one night, square go at the bar, a straight'ner. Two big men, beasts really, ready to tear limbs and snap bones to save honour. Amazin'. Twenty Neck should never 'ave even been in the club in the first place. I admit that. He should never 'ave got through the doors. I still can't believe he got past me. It's rare that a turd'll get past my shit detectors but, well, he seemed all right when he came in. Even 'ad a chat with me. I thought he was OK. Then 'e got a few of them down him and, well, you know the crack, suddenly 'e's got this fucking ugly head on. Soon as he started I told 'im, 'You'll 'ave to leave if you don't wind your neck in,' but he wouldn't have any of it. I had a word with the heavy artillery, Killer Kenny, the one-man-gang. Kenny says, 'You should 'ave dealt with it, Tony.' He 'ad to go. The man was a liability, a tyrant, serving his own drinks, intimidatin' the staff, scarin' the arm candy. The usual nightclub despot kind of guy that keeps a fella in work.

So Kenny corners him by the bar and lines 'im up with a right. 'You've gotta leave.' Twenty Neck weren't 'avin' any of it. 'If you want me out,' he goes, 'You get me out!' Well, that was about the stupidest thing 'e could 'ave said. Told Kenny everything 'e needed to know. The interview was over. Let the battle commence, as

Doorman

they say. Not one to rush a job, Kenny touches his glass hand like this – (*shows*) – to see what 'e'd got. If they let you touch their drinking hand you know they're not serious. If they snatch it back like that – (*shows*) – you know it's on. Anyway, Kenny touched the glass hand and said, 'So you're not gonna go then?' He said it dead quiet like, makes 'em think your arsehole's gone man-hole.

The place was herded with bodies. All the punters made a circle around them, like a booth fight. Very smoky. Twenty Neck snatched his hand back. 'Get the fuck off m' beer.' Only he never got it all out... BANG! Kenny plugged 'im with a left hand 'n' gave him the bad news. He hit him so hard he went back in time; when he woke up his clothes was out of fuckin' fashion. He hit the floor so hard all the glasses jumped off the tables and everyone started clapping and cheering – even the women. I couldn't believe it. They were actually clapping. They know the crack, though, they know a good punch when they see one. Mind you, the women we get in here are rough, you spend most of your time looking for an Adam's apple.

We have this one Doris in regular. Big girl, swede like that fucker – (*shows*) – face like a Toby Jug. One ear up there

21

like that – (*shows*) – and the other down here like that
fucker (*shows*). Anyway, I'm dead nice to 'er, try to look
after 'er, you know, 'ave the crack, 'cos everyone else treats
her like a troll.

One night I says to her, 'How ya doin'? Cor, give us a
kiss, I 'aven't seen you since the Dead Sea was still only
ill.' Strange girl, got a fixation for very fit men, know
what I'm sayin'? (*Flexes his muscles*) Very fit men. She
goes, 'I'm a runner, me. Used to run for the county.'
'Oh yeah?' I goes. I looks her up and down. Big girl.
Huge legs, huge, beasts, calves like Spanish wine
bottles. She looked illegal in leggings. I couldn't see no
runner... unless she'd swallowed one. I goes, 'Last thing
you ran for, love, was the ice cream van.' Fuck me, that
didn't go down very well, sensitive cow starts attacking
me. Dead sensitive, women, ain't they? I said, 'I'm only
jokin', you bag of sick, I'm only jokin'. What are you
like? 'Ave a word with yourself, I'm fishin', reeling you
in. I'm just 'avin a gag with ya. Go on, fuck off, get
yourself in the club before I shag you where you stand.'
Fuck, ain't women touchy? I'm just glad I never
mentioned the moustache. Fucking Mexican.

Anyway, so Kenny's sparked this Twenty Neck
character, he's splashed across the carpet like a come-

Doorman

stain. Kenny goes 'Get 'im out', but we couldn't move 'im, could we, we couldn't shift the fat fucker. He was heavier than a dead politician. We just couldn't lift 'im. So Radio Rental Rob – crazy fucker, just finished a five for a Section 18 with intent, the guy he jobbed up looked like he'd been hit-and-runned – 'e moved all the tables out of the way, and we rolls him out the back doors. Laugh? I thought I was gonna bust me corset. We dumped him round by the bins with the other rubbish and turned him onto his side; the recovery position. Stops 'em from choking.

Depending on how hard you hit 'em and how much they've had to drink, they normally come round on their own. If not, we sit them up, slap their faces, shout at them. If they're really bad Rob even gives them a squirt with the fire extinguisher. That wakes the fuckers. We have to see them conscious before we close the doors, you know what I'm sayin', otherwise it's on your mind all night. You don't want the fuckers dying on ya. You're looking at fifteen minimum if you corpse them. It's not good for the club. We're paid to protect the licence. If they're really bad we call an ambulance, but it has to be bad 'cos that means a visit from plod, which is the last thing you need.

Doorman

If we're feeling a bit mischievous, you know, a bit naughty, we might get the wings out. What we do, right, is we wait until they start to stir then we get these angel wings left over from a fancy dress party, then we get the DJ – Slippery Deck, gayer than a seventies musical, a right gay thing – we get him to put the dry ice smoke on full so that it's pouring out of the exit doors, then we stand there, dressed like a couple of heavenly cherubs surrounded by clouds of smoke. As soon as they open their eyes – when they wake up they're like babies for the first few seconds, they don't know where the fuck they are, in fact sometimes they don't even know who they are – the minute their eyes open we start this fucker – (*shows*) – 'Ohhhhh, ohhhhhh', we start hovering and making ghost noises.

The look on their faces, it's a picture, I'm tellin' ya, the fear comes out of them in chunks. They crap their nappies, mouths ajar like a cartoon cat, then we drift back into the smoke and close the doors. They're outside running around screaming and we're in the club pissing ourselves.

We don't do it to them all, just the ones that need a bit of fright. Does the trick too, sorts them right out I can tell you. We had one guy – a proper gangster, proper

24

Doorman

granite, you know what I mean, a real hard case – we
gave 'im the wings and it retired him, honest, found
God and everything. Last I heard he was singing gospel
and selling Bibles door to door.

This crack's not for everyone, though, not everyone
gets it. The violence, I mean. I understand that. I do,
honestly, and I don't mind that you don't get it, I really
don't. But, in my opinion, someone's gotta do it,
someone's got to shovel the shit, and just 'cos you don't
like the smell don't mean it's gonna go away.

'God and the bouncer all men adore,
In times of trouble but not before,
When the enemy's gone and the wrong is righted,
God is forgotten and the bouncer slighted.'

Read that somewhere about soldiers, I just changed the
words a bit to suit but I think it says the same about us.
People like me. We're damned if we do and damned if
we fucking well don't.

Like this guy I weighed in last week, as a for-instance. I
chins this guy outside the club, right, gave 'im a little
left off the front leg – (*shows*) – beautiful shot, caught
'im right on the point of the jaw, timed it lovely, landed

just as he was doin' the old, 'I'm gonna come back for you.'

I 'ate it when these fuckers say they're gonna come back. What's that all about? What is that all a-fuckin'-bout? Don't come back, do it now. Now! 'E's out like the gas an' I goes into me talkin'-to-unconscious-people routine. 'Gonna come back for me are ya,' I says, only 'e's not answerin' on account of the fact that he's fuckin' unconscious, out like a baby, in sleepsville. 'Gonna fuckin' come back? You wanna piece of this, do ya?' Like he's gonna answer me back. Layin' there like a corpse and I'm havin' the chat with 'im. The man's fuckin' *out there* and I'm 'avin a conversation. (*Bends over an imaginary, prostrate opponent, and points in his face as he speaks*) 'Gonna come back are ya, y' fuckin' lemon, gonna fuckin' come back?' (*Stands back up*) Fuckers oughta think before they start threatening to come back on me.

Then this Doris appears out of nowhere, in me face like that – (*shows*) – and the breath on it, she goes, 'You're a fuckin' animal!' I says, 'It's very nice of you to say so.' Well, did I 'it the jackpot or what. Next thing you know she's wrappin' her stiletto round me ear'ole screamin', 'Violence is not the answer! Violence is not the answer!'

Doorman

while she's trying to lobotomise me with the heel of her right shoe. I mean, you tell me. It wouldn't be so bad but – and this is what I was talkin' about earlier, the irony – the guy I chinned only got it 'cos he broke some Doris' nose in the club 'cos she wouldn't dance with 'im. What would you do if some spoon abused your little girl? Broke her nose. Made her bleed. Your little girl. Your baby. Pissin' with blood 'cos she said no to a dance. They'd 'ave to call a surgeon to cut your fingers from his throat. Am I right?

We're all someone's kids. They're all someone's babies. I'm not sayin' you're wrong, because I don't think you are. Neither of us is wrong. It's just that I'm seein' it from this side of the door and you're seeing it from that side. We're both lookin' at different narratives. Like that guy earlier, the one I weighed in. I saw a threat, you saw a victim. I used... semi-control, but you saw abuse.

And me, look at me. I look in a mirror and see a nice bloke trapped in a dark trade. What do you see? When you look at me what do you see? I bet you struggle to get beyond the dicky bow. I bet most of you don't even see a member of the same fucking species. And why should ya? We don't speak the same tongue. We might as well be from different planets.

Doorman

It's funny, though, at the pictures you love it, love it,
you actually pay to see it. You watch torture and death
through mouthfuls of popcorn and handfuls of tit and
then cheer because you get it. Some guy's been
cornered by the coffin, 'e's deader than Darwin and
you're dead happy 'cos you get it. You're clever fuckers.
You get the writer's subtle wit, the director's irony, even
that the baddie is paying a karmic debt for something
he did earlier in the film.

And of course the coup de grâce, the lead through the
eye, is delivered by some catalogue clothes horse,
y'know what I'm sayin', some good lookin' fucker. It's
OK to blow some fucker's swede apart as long as the
trigger hand is attached to a catalogue John. When
Travolta shoots that guy in the head in *Pulp Fiction*, by
accident, in the back of the car. Everyone cracks up.
Blood and bits of brain and snot and teeth decorating
the back seat of the car and we're gagging on our
popcorn. What's that all about? I mean, if that were for
real you'd be in therapy. You'd be keeping some head
doctor in BMWs for the next decade.

Beat. **Tony** *smiles.*

Doorman

Perhaps I should get Travolta to do a shift here.
D'y'reckon he'd do it for fifty a night?

Beat.

I think he got an Oscar for that 'n' all. I doubt if I'll get
a nomination for tonight's performance. (*Looks at
watch*) Two o'clock. Time to get 'em out.

Boom-boom music as **Tony** *settles himself down at the table
and chair enjoying an after hours drink and some crisps. The
music fades out.* **Tony** *pats his ears and shakes his head as
though trying to clear the noise.*

Boom Boom fuckin' Boom. The music's off, the DJ's
at home getting his bottom spunked, the punters are in
bed catchin' forty and that racket is still ragin' in my
head, it's stuck like chewing gum. Still, got me half a
lager and a bag of smoky bacon crisps. Nirvana. Doesn't
get any better than this, let me tell ya. Chilled glass of
beer and a bag of Walkers. What more can a fella ask
for? Gives me a chance to wind me neck in.

I like a chance to get the violence out of me, otherwise
it starts spilling over into me real life. I used to hate
violence, me, 'ate it. I was bullied at school. Yeah, me!

Doorman

No duff. I'm bein' straight. You wouldn't know it,
would ya? I wasn't always built like Desperate Dan.
Even the girls used to chase me 'ome from school. I
was like a little tart, I even looked like a Doris. Me
mum and dad spent the first half of me life worrying
that I'd top meself. Felt like it once or twice. 'Alf the
time I was too scared to even go to school, if I'm bein'
honest, used to cry in me mum's cardy and beg her to
let me stay home. She reckons I inherited her nerves.
Lonely times.

I suppose that's why I ended up 'ere, to face it down.
Fear. The murky corner dweller that put skid-marks in
me Y-fronts. Like that guy with the whale in Moby
Dick. I can still remember my very first night on the
door. Scared? I'd never felt fear like it. Knee-deep in the
brown stuff. A virgin to violence. Now I'm an old
slapper, in a manner of speaking. I was dead surprised,
too. About the fear. Dead surprised. I thought I was the
only one. Turns out every fucker feels it, although most
don't like to admit it.

Don't get me wrong, I'm not complainin'. I'm here out
of choice. The door's been good to me. Got me a good
wedge, plenty of respect. The odd shag. Wasn't 'ard to
get the job. Only one question on the application form:

Doorman

'Can you have a fight?' Not too taxing, I have to say. No CV needed, no references, other than maybe a current criminal record. No, just a simple solitary question:

'Can-you-fuckin'-ave-it?'

'Yes.'

'You've got the job. When can you start?'

'Now!'

'Good, there's a woolly mammoth helping himself to drinks at the bar – ask him to leave.'

And let me tell ya, there 'ave been a few woolly mammoths since I started here, and not all of the male variety.

If I'm honest I like the notoriety, the fame. I like walking into a club to whispers and nudges, recognition, admiration, a line of free beers along the bar like winners' cups. It makes you feel like somebody. I like looking in the mirror and liking the man that looks back. (*Fiddles with bloody sock*) I hate this bit, though; you can't get the fucker out once it's settled. By the time I get 'ome it'll be like crusty gussets. It'll grate at me nerves. It won't be the first time I've left here with only one sock on, let me tell ya. It doesn't matter that you can't see it, I know it's there. When I used to go home to her with one sock missin' she'd rare up, 'Where's your fuckin' sock, 'ave you been shaggin'?' 'Yeah, course I have. I used the sock as a nodder and 'ad to sling it afterwards to hide the evidence.' Stupid fucker! I can just hear the headlines on News at Ten, 'Police were puzzled today when they discovered dozens of black cotton socks, apparently filled with semen.'

It's a fucker to get out. Blood. The amount of clothes I've 'ad to bin because some sloppy spanner decided to bleed on me. Found a tooth stuck to me sock one night, straight up, a fuckin' tooth. It was a shock, I have to say. I mean, it's the last place you expect to find a tooth. Attached to your right sock. Kicked it right out of some psycho's head. Big gapin' hole where his teeth should have been, lumps of flesh hangin' over his chin, blood gushin' out all over the place. 'Is missus – pretty little thing – she's trying to catch it all in a bit of tissue. She was sobbin' her heart out. She kept screamin' at me, 'Why? Why? Why?' It's 'cos he was a right lippy fucker,

Doorman

that's why. Should've put a gate on his mouth, then I wouldn't've 'ad t' plug 'im. 'S no big shakes, it was only a tooth – well, teeth; we found a few more in the blood when we Dettol'd it later. Teeth don't look right when they're not attached to gums.

For months afterwards I could feel that fuckin' tooth. No matter 'ow many new pairs of socks she got me I could still feel it stuck right here. (*Shows*) Strange. And blood! She used to scrub them in the sink 'til they were Persil white, *Persil* white. But I could still see it knitted into the fibres. She'd go – not that she knew anythin' about what I 'ave to put up with 'ere, what with bein' a bull's-eye for every fucker who stubbed their toe or lost a button. She knew more about rocket science, in fact she wouldn't even say it was work: 'That's not work, it's a piss up with your mates.' She used to do my head right in.

Anyway that's another story, I don't want to bore you with the histrionics of my marriage. She'd be holding the sock up to the light goin', 'There's nothin' there!' Nothin' there! Nothing fuckin' there. I grabbed her by the nightie: 'It's fuckin' covered in blood, it's drippin', you stupid cunt. Chuck it in the bin, get it out of me sight, it's there – can't y' feel it, can't y' smell it, can't y'

Doorman

fuckin' hear it jumpin' from thread to thread?' Then she'd wash it again and again, but it don't make no difference; once the fucker's on ya there's no washin' it off.

See, that's the thing, that's what people don't realise, they don't get it. You don't just 'ave a fight and that's the end of it. You can't just knock 'em out and then put the situation neatly to bed. It don't work like that, it don't. There's more to it than just having a fight. Fighting's not hard. A fuckin' monkey could do it. 'S like fallin' off a log. This is the real arena – (*taps head*) – dealin' with your 'ead. See, she didn't get that, she just thought it was like working a fucking lathe from nine to five, come 'ome, 'ave your tea, go for a pint, back for a shag, blah-dee-fuckin' blah.

This is quantum leaps from the factory. Y' can't switch the lathe off in 'ere – (*taps head*) – it's a permanent fixture, 24-7, it's like, like, I can't even go for a fuckin' piss without 'avin' to worry about my back – d'ya realise 'ow vulnerable you are with your dick out? Don't bear thinkin' about. I have to go in the cubicle and lock the door before the piss'll even consider vacating me bladder. You think I'm jestin'? No lock, no piss.

Doorman

Do you like to eat out? I love it but it did her swede right in. Restaurants? She used to go Hatton. She'd say – and this is all 'cos I wouldn't eat me snap 'til me back was up a wall and I'm sat so's I can see the door, y'know, who's comin' in, who's leavin', that kind of stuff – she'd go, 'You're doolally-tip, you, you'll end up in Hatton.' I'm not an 'ead-the-ball, just careful.

Mind you, sometimes she did 'ave a point. Once this waiter – was it a waiter or a punter? Don't matter, anyway, whoever it was dropped a glass. That's right, it was a waiter 'cos she said the bloke couldn't work for the rest of the night afterwards. Yeah, this waiter, 'e's walkin' past our table, minding his own business when *crash*! 'E's dropped a glass on the floor, by accident, obviously, but I wasn't to know that. I mean, as far as I was concerned we was back in the club and a fight was kicking off – see, that's one of the first signs of a row, the sound of breakin' glass. I 'ear that fucker in me sleep.

So anyway, the glass has hit the deck – crash! Bang! I'm out of me chair, mouth full of meat, head-locking the guy and dragging him from the restaurant – his own fuckin' restaurant – by the neck. His little legs are kicking out, he's gagging for breath – I've got 'im round the throat, it always makes 'em gag – and before I know what I'm doin' the guy's on the pavement on his back with me hovering over him like the woolly mammoth. Well the lad was as pale as a Russian swimmer. I looked down and all of a sudden this wet patch appears round his bollocks and down his leg, and steam started rising from his trousers.

Course, once I realised 'e was a waiter I was dead apologetic, tried to help 'im up an' everythin', but when I reached me 'and towards him he cowered and started to cry. There was no need for that, it was an accident for fuck's sake, 's not as though I did it on purpose. I felt dead bad for 'im.

Well that fucked the night right up the rivet. She started raring up, the manager called the police, I got lifted and spent the night in the cells, released with a caution. They couldn't charge me, I didn't actually hit 'im. That cost me a week of microwave dinners and a cold back in bed. So, we didn't do restaurants any more. Surprisingly.

See that's what I'm sayin', there's more to this job than working a lathe. It's learnin' to control your thoughts, handlin' the consequences. There's a price that goes

Doorman

with bein' able to 'ave a fight. Comebacks, police involvement, prison, the 2 a.m. phone call: 'See, you son, you're calendar material. I'm gonna kill your wife and your kids.'

You have to deal with it. You have to swat nagging thoughts like flies, you have to control the voices otherwise they become ya. Killer Kenny says, 'Tony, you've got to treat your head like the club. Put a bouncer on your swede. Stop the shit at the door. If y' fuck up an' it gets in, drag it back out by the throat. An' don't take any bollocks! It's your 'ead, if you don't want somethin' in there, fuck it off out.'

Tony *takes a drink from his glass*

Ahh, staff drinks, this is the bit I like. 'Alf a lager and a bag of smoky bacon crisps. Fuckin' mint. They're all right 'ere, 'eads in orbit though, y' know, out there, but besides that they're all right. Take Jean, as a for-instance, she's a good girl, no, she is, she's sound, looks after the coats in the cloakroom. Although she's only stayin' for a bit, she's got aspirations. Yeah, now there's a luxury. She's not here with us now, she's not hanging coats and makin' tea, she's not taking drunken abuse from some wanker who's lost his coat ticket. No, she's semi-clad and *haute couture* on a Paris

Doorman

catwalk pouting to the world's press. Listen, I've seen the portfolio, there's more than a passing resemblance to Eric Bristow.

It's funny, though, innit? Don't you think, don't you think it's dead funny, one of them ironies? No one's ever staying. No one's ever fuckin' stayin', they're all just passing through on their way to somethin' better. Ten years, a mortgage and a rake of shitty nappies later and they still haven't fuckin' moved.

Don't get me wrong, there's nothing wrong with aspiration, nothing wrong at all. In fact, I heartily recommend it. I reckon they should give it away on the back of a cornflake box. I wish they'd've given me aspiration at the comprehensive instead of PE and a list of local factories looking for lathe turners and bog cleaners. If they had I might not 'ave ended up 'ere. Not for much longer though. I've got me own plans. I'm passing through as well, difference is I'll do it. I won't be hanging round waiting for providence to knock on my door. I know I'm sounding all cynical and judgmental, but really, I'm not against it, I just tire of hearing it through the bottom of a beer glass.

Doorman

Most of them fuckers cabbage me, they carry their aspiration in a beer bag that hangs over their belt like a balcony. You wouldn't mind if they did other than talk about it. If they spent a bit more time doing and a bit less time saying, they'd get a lot less said and a lot more fuckin' done. If you get my meaning. Tonight they're full of beer; they'll chase the stars around the Galaxy. Tomorrow? They'll chase dog ends down the piss trough at the factory. That's the truth of it and the truth don't lie.

Take Thick Mick, covers on Mondays, he's a contender, contender no less. A boxer, a pugilist, a gloved fighter of repute, a serial brain cell killer, a man that thrashes the fuck out of another man in a circus ring while fat, cheering businessmen chomp on lumps of dead cow. Ladies and gentlemen I give you the one, the only, the future heavyweight champion of the world – once he's earned enough money to train full-time and learned to box, because at the moment the lad couldn't box fuckin' eggs. Micky-The-Jabber Jones. But hey, the money he earns here just about keeps him in flesh. And anyway, who can blame him? He'll tell ya it's not his fault. After working here all night he ain't got the energy left to train. Innit strange that when people fail it's never their fault? It's never down to them.

Doorman

But I suppose they could do worse. Here is as good as anywhere. If it ain't the blood and snot and bullshit of the beer house it's the oil and noise of the factory. No one wants it. They don't! They all say they're content but they're not, they're just fuckin' safe. When we were kids we swore never to settle for it. We promised ourselves. I remember watching me dad come back through the gate at six o'clock every night covered in shit and stinking of oil and thinking, 'I'm not gonna do that.' But where I come from, dreams of flying to the moon and kicking a football get clubbed like a beached seal. You take the bus to the factory straight from the comprehensive. Y' get your nails full of shit by dinnertime and learn the art of procrastination by tea. The work's dirty, it's 'orrible, the language and dinner table porn are dirtier still, but the filthiest bastard of all is the foreman who keeps you at the lathe with the threat of the dole line. Not me, I'm not 'avin' any of it.

Y' know, I look around me – and she 'ated it when I got like this 'cos she reckoned I should've been grateful for even 'avin' a job – I look around me and all I see are postponed lives, everyone's livin' for the lottery finger. But it don't point at people like us. Sometimes it looks like it's gonna, then right at the last minute it does this fucker – (*shows the 'up yours' finger*) – am I right or am I right? I'm right, en I? And then this little sign comes up and says, 'It could be you... but it fuckin' well ain't so sit on it.' (*Sound of police sirens in the background.*) Hear that? That's my lottery.

The police sirens get louder, mixing with the boom-boom of the music. **Tony** *moves over to the bench. The music and sirens fade out.*

I won't be 'ere long. (*Pulls up his right trouser leg showing that he has no sock on*) No evidence. (*He leans back, hands behind his head arrogantly*) Like the room, do ya? What more could a fella ask for? En-suite. Great view. And when plod starts flinging drunks downstairs we might even get a bit of entertainment.

This is the thanks I get for whacking the head off that psycho. This is my reward for cleaning the shit off society's shoe. My own little Oscar. No doubt they'll try 'n' drag me to Crown. That'll be a fucking laugh. I can see it now, some fuckin' coffin-dodger rubbing his well-groomed chin with manicured fingers that've never seen a callus saying, 'You knocked this gentleman unconscious and kicked him how many times?' It won't get that far. Before y' man's head even hit the pavement I had three witnesses who'll swear on their mothers' graves that my hands never even left my pockets.

That's the crack. If you want to avoid the big house you've got to know the crack. I understand the law, I use the law, I fuck the law. I know it like me own foreskin. And they fuckin' 'ate me because they know that I know. People like me are not convicted for what they do, they're convicted for what they say. So I'm dead fuckin' careful about the words that tumble from these lips. And what I leave behind. If they go to the club now alls they'll find is a mop full of Dettol and three wise monkeys. They know I did it, every fucker knows I did it, but they can't pin it on me because I know the crack and they know I know. They'll keep me in here all night without a blanket or a phone call. I'll ring that bell but they won't answer. That's the game. That's their little way of punishing me because they know they've got to let me go. I stick a bit of paper in the bell so they 'ave to listen to it ring all fuckin' night. It'll cabbage them. That's my little way of punishing them. Take my word for it, the charge will be dropped.

That's not to say everyone escapes the big house. Those that don't know the law do the time. Lenny Five Years – 'e just got life for his third 18, fucking head-the-ball, by

Doorman

the way, of the first order, violent by proxy. Seen 'im
put five away one night with a beer jug and a penknife.
Masterful. The Bill Gates of violence. Tattoos! I've
never seen so many, he's like a walking canvas of blue
ink art. And piercings – he's actually got a bull-ring
through his dick. He says it really improves his sex life
and now he can piss in five directions at the same time.
And he's got AIDS tattooed along the shaft. It's true,
I've seen it. Only when he gets a hard-on it says
ADIDAS. So I've been told.

Terry Two Ears – oh fuck me, that lad can 'ave a fight.
And funny, I can't even begin to tell ya. Great bloke.
'E's doin' an eight for attempted murder on three tit-
hats. Unpredictable fucker, though; never sit next to
him when he's got a sniffy bugle, know what I'm sayin',
or you'll find yourself wearing a broken glass. Fuckin'
psycho. I remember the time 'e glassed 'is missus, 'is
own missus, hole in her face like that fucker – (*shows*) –
gapin' wound, you could fit four fingers into it.
Hideous. Slaughtered her looks – poor girl 'ardly ever
leaves the 'ouse now. 'E reckons that's the way 'e likes
it. Then there's Mad Mickey, of course, definitely out
there, currently remanded awaiting sentence for trying
to cut some fucker's nose off with a dessert spoon.

Doorman

Yeah, you've got to know the crack. I've been involved in more woundings than any bouncer I know, but I've never spent more than one night in a cell. No fibs. It's not so bad, though, once you get accustomed. It's safe, warm. It's not the Ritz but hey, you've got to be grateful for any security you can get these days.

That's what my old dad used to tell me... when he wasn't chasing the coffin with the sherry bottle... before his liver shrunk t' the size of a cornflake. Never forget the old man, me, in that hospital bed, chest rasping like a fuckin' accordion, grapplin' for every breath. Yella skin... eyes like egg yokes... looked like fuckin' Yoda... and 'is belly, fuck me, like that. (*Shows*) Distended, they said. Pregnant more like. Left 'is kidneys down the pub. I told 'im the drink'd kill 'im, told 'im 'e should think of me mum, and the grandkids but 'e just kept lacin' it down 'im like 'e was in a race. Selfish bastard! I just kept crying.

Anyway, 's all right to cry. Me mum reckons that's my problem, I don't let it out enough. 'You're the sensitive one,' she says, 'But y' keep your feelings caged, then when they finally do come out somebody gets ravaged.'

Doorman

Talkin' about lettin' it out, that fuckin' racket's still stuck in my swede. Boom fuckin' Boom. 'S like there's an amplifier stuck in me head.

It's the loneliness that gets to me most when they're banged up in here. It's about the only time they're ever forced to spend a night with some fucker they can't stand. People don't like their own company. This place makes them look in the honest mirror. Usually they see some horrible bastard that they don't even recognise staring right back at them. It can do your head right in.

They leave you on your own, see, them fuckers, in the dark. In the cold. Hours, with nothin' but rogue thoughts for company. They crowd your head 'til it throbs, little dwarf assassins daggering, daggering. And it's normally thoughts they plant in your head as they bang you away. 'You do realise the seriousness of this? You know you're looking at an eight?' Crafty fuckers. They're not stupid. They always used to try and two me up with some drunken bastard, just to cabbage me, but I told them, 'You put that piss ant in here with me and I'll send the fucker out in a box.' They never bothered after that. They know the crack. They're not stupid. They know that a couple of hours of 'jail' racing around your swede, a couple of hours thinking about doin' time, thinkin' about bein' away, they know it'll cabbage ya. That's the whole idea, leave you on your own, let your head run away with itself then *bang*. They come in when you're vulnerability's like an open wound and offer to let you go home, but only if you'll confess. By that time you're so desperate you'd admit to the fuckin' Brink's bank robbery if you thought it might get you home.

It don't work with me. I've heard it too many times. I don't 'ave any of it. It's hard, though. You have to get your head around it dead quick. Once the leechy thoughts are in they suck ya dry. With me it's the kids. You wanna see my kids, they're beautiful. Gorgeous little things. Only that big. (*Shows*) I often wonder what'd 'appen if I did get eight. I'd miss practically all their childhood. It's the thought of them cryin' for me. I can see myself chasing them around the park laughing and giggling. My kids love the bones off me. They do.

See. That's the very thoughts I'm talkin' about. As hard as it is, you've gotta push them out. For as long as I'm in here I've got no kids. I know that sounds hard, it 'urts to even think about it, but honestly, I have to do it otherwise my brain'll feel like it's been put through a blender by the end of the night. Your resolve'll go all fluid at the knees. It's only for one night. Y' can stand anythin' for one night. (*Pause*) Got a picture of 'em. 'E took it off me when I came in. The Sergeant. Lard Arse. He goes, 'How do you feel knowing that you're not going to see them for eight years?' Done my head right in. I never let 'im see it, though. I wouldn't give him the satisfaction. Fat fucker. E's 'orrible as bastards, a mouth full of tartar. Hairs 'anging from his nose that your kids could swing off. And the arse on him. Like that fucker. (*Shows*) Y' could play a game of five-a-side soccer in them pants. I said to 'im, 'Keep the picture, it's the closest you'll ever get to 'avin kids.' Ohh, fuck me, that 'it a nerve. Went crazy, big red head on him, veins poppin' out like fuckin' scaffold poles. I thought he was gonna pop.

You can't let them get to you. Better to think about emotionless things like the tiles on the floor. How many across? Eight. How many in length? Thirteen. How many in total? 104. How many tiles broken? Four. What's the percentage of broken tiles? (*Tries to work it out*) Haven't got a fuckin' clue. Then I'll count the bricks in each wall. Across, down, total. Then I'll do some press-ups. (*Does some*) Sit-ups. (*Does some*) Burpees. (*Does some*) Stretching. (*Does some*) Shadow boxing. (*Does some, then lies back on bench.*) Keeps my mind busy, and it gets the adrenaline out of me.

Makes it easier to sleep.

'S like fallin' off a log.

Boom-boom music. **Tony** *changes the position of the chair. He is carrying a plastic carrier bag. The music fades out.*

Home sweet home. Could do with a lick of paint. Bedsit land.

Looks at his watch. He produces a pork pie, a carton of milk and a Pot Noodle from the bag and puts them on the table.

Four in the mornin', I'm out. Told ya, didn't I? They've got nothin' on me. I thought Lard Arse was gonna cry. He said 'I've got a long memory.' I said, 'Not as long as your face, you sad bastard.' Pork pies and Pot Noodles, the staple diet of a single man. Not that I was always single. Before the decree nisi drilled me up the arse, I ate like a king: full English breakfast, cooked meals on the table when I came home from work every night – she never did learn to put it on a plate. She was a great cook though, she could really lay on a feast.

Doorman

Beat

I lived that lie for nine years. Nine years. That's what they give y' for murder. Nine years with a beautiful girl that turned into a hard-faced cow. Let me tell ya, it's no fun being a spousal punchbag. Neither is waking up next to a bed full of flesh that you no longer recognise. A farting stranger masquerading as the girl you once worshipped. In the end I couldn't stand being near her. She made m' skin crawl. Even the door was better than bein' at home listening to all that nag. Sex? I've never necked so many aspirins. It's funny how someone who used to bring out your best starts to bring out your worst. She'd start this -(*mimics nagging with hand*) – I'd rare up, she'd attack me with m' dinner, I'd slap 'er, the kids'd run round the house screamin', then I'd bugger off to the pub and take solace from the pint glass and me same-ilk mates. Then she'd blank me 'til I apologised. Which I'd do in the end 'cos I hated the silence. The violence of silence I called it. She used it to punish me. I'd rather fight Tyson than rattle round my own house with a conjugal fatwa on my head. I used to apologise sometimes, whether it was my fault or not. Anything for a quiet life, just to get it back to normal again.

Doorman

Sometimes I'd look for her when she was asleep. I'd
stare at her looking for any old resemblance. She was
just a sweet little thing when I met her. Beautiful.
Oriental features, hourglass figure, great shag.
Attentive. Do anythin' for me. Anythin'! Great shag.
Did I say that? She was a dream, I'm not kidding, I was
besotted.

She got dead fat. She did. She used to be like that when
I met her – (*shows*) – like a knittin' needle, she was that
thin. (*Shows*) I could get me fingers round 'er waist. A
few years of fish 'n' chip suppers swilled down with a
barrel of contentment and she's built like a bottle bank.
Big floppy arms that knock cups off tables. It's 'ow I
felt. It cabbaged me, no fibs. Maybe it's just me, I don't
know, but urrrgh! Did nothin' for me. And you don't
notice it happening. There's no subtle signs, no steady
build up, no gentle hints or winks or nudges. You don't
get a blue letter then a red letter then a final reminder,
you don't, you just wake up one day and bang! Y'
married to Jabba the fuckin' Hutt! It's a shock. Hits
you. And it's the scariest feeling. Scary. Knowin' that
you don't love her any more, that you've got to leave,
but at the same time knowing that it's going to hit her
like an axe, because she still loves the bones off you.

Doorman

I cried when I left. I had to go. Me mate Barney said – 'e's a bit of a philosopher – he said – and 'e should know, 'e's been through a rake of women – 'e said, 'T-T-Tony.' He had a bit of a stutter did Barney, took him about an hour to tell punters they couldn't come in if they had trainers on. Actually, 'e was a bit of a liability but we kept 'im on 'cos he could 'ave a fight. He said, 'T-T-T-Tony, women are like back gardens, every now and then they need a good dig.' Must be summat in it; that theory has taken 'im through four marriages.

Yeah, I cried when I left. Blarted like a nipper. I hurt her so much. I know I did. I'll never forget the pain in her face. She was a shell. I couldn't believe how frail, how vulnerable she looked. She knew it'd gone. That was the hardest part. She knew. I didn't even have to tell her. It couldn't be brought back. I hurt her. I regret that. I had to go. Me kids cried their eyes out. Thought I was abandoning them. I suppose I was. I said I wasn't. But I was. I said it'd be better for them, said the arguing wasn't good for them and at least if me and mum was apart they'd get to see us both at our best. Usual bollocks that you make up to try an' rationalise deserting people.

Doorman

I don't know who I was trying to convince, them or me. Deserting people! Never saw meself as a deserter. I wanted my freedom. I wanted to be eighteen. They stood on the doorstep, my babies, little arms out like that – (*shows*) – trying to fetch me back. 'I'm not leaving ya, I'm just nippin' to the shops, I'll be back just now.' They knew I was lyin'. Followed me all the way down the street. Promised I'd go back weekends. And I did. For a bit. Livin' on your own, out on the town, shaggin' everythin' with a pulse, you sort of forget you're a dad. It's like you left your responsibilities in another jacket. You forget. It hurts less that way. 'Til they ring cryin' 'cos you missed their birthday or y' forgot their school play or summat.

'S funny how the women get dumped with the kids and the men end up makin' excuses about why they're always busy at the weekend. She goes, 'I hope you find what you're looking for, Tony.' She was dead nice about it, considerin'. That didn't last long, though. Within a week she was back to her old self. I was the biggest scum fuck that ever crawled the earth. She tried to run me over with my own Cortina. My own car. Would you... I couldn't... I loved that car. Then she stopped me from seeing the kids. Didn't want them being round violence. She said blokes shouldn't hit women...

not in front of kids, anyway. That was worse than the Cortina across the ankles. She shouldn't 'ave used the kids. 'You hurt me,' she said. 'Now I'm gonna hurt you any way I can.'

She did hurt me, too. I went for them for the first few weeks but, well you know 'ow it is, she rared up a couple of times, then I stopped tryin' and blamed her. I was always good at that. Blamin'. Trouble is once you start, the blamin' never ends. Once I was gone she used every weakness she'd learned about me over the last decade, most of which I'd told her when we were in the pit. Ohh, she was good too, clinical, a surgeon, cut me to bits. My kids... my babies... they was her biggest weapon. First she wouldn't let me see them, then she was dumping them on me doorstep saying, 'You're 'avin them,' then she'd take them back again and tell *them* to choose. They didn't know whether they were coming or going.

Beat

I'm comin' off the door. I've had enough. I'm tired of the violence. Tired. It's not like you can even leave the grief at the club, you take it home with ya. There's no escape. For one, there's the constant threat of comeback. I carry a weapon everywhere. When I was back home, every room was equipped with a tool. Just in case. Every room. You think I'm paranoid? My ex thought so too when I placed a samurai by the front door and a shiv in the shit-house.

Taking security precautions is a lesson hard learned. I ain't gonna get caught out like Steve. Excellent boxer, he could really 'ave a fight. But it didn't help him. He had a run-in with some heavies. They threatened to do a 'house call'. He should have taken precautions. He didn't. The three brothers paid him a visit one quiet Sunday afternoon. I mean, who would expect it? Sunday after a few pints at the local, dozing in front of the telly, hand full of tit when CRASH! CRASH! CRASH! The front door's hoofed down and he's suddenly yanked from his chair by six arms and dragged to the floor. On his back, feet stomping his head into the carpet. This wasn't a slap, they wanted to kill him. One of them dragged Steve's missus out of the room by the hair and gave her a beastin'. Pregnant as well. Then 'e grabs a cast-iron saucepan and an iron from the kitchen. While the other two held Steve down, he smashed all his fingers until the bones snapped and stuck through the skin. The room was drenched in blood. His missus screaming in the other room, baby gushin' through her knickers. *Songs of Praise* on the TV in the background.

There's an irony. He tried to fight back, he tried to get up, but every time he tried the saucepan or the iron was smashed across his nose and teeth. They wanted to beat him to death. They kicked his eyes with the toes of their boots until they looked like two plums. One of them shouted, 'Get me a knife! Get me a knife! I'm gonna cut his arse!' So they get a serrated jobby from the kitchen.

Beat

Steve died in the ambulance. They smashed his face so bad his mum didn't know him. 'Ad to call in his dentist for a proper ID. Every joint on his body was smashed until it swelled to twice its normal size. I see violence everywhere. In everything. I line everyone up as a matter of course. Everyone. I was with me mum the other day – listen to this and you'll know why I have to come off the door, and in a hurry. Took me mum shopping. Tescos. We were half way down the fruit aisle, talking about the benefits of fresh over tinned peach when suddenly – and I don't know how it came about – suddenly I found myself lining her up. Me

Doorman

mum. I was linin' her up for a right cross. She reckons I should see a trick-cyclist. I can't. just can't.

Anyway, that's past. I'm here now with all I own in the world and I've never been happier. This room might smell of piss, it might have a leaky sink and dodgy wiring and neighbours that look like serial killers, but to me it's freedom, it's liberty, a fresh start, great adventure, new opportunities. (*Bites pork pie.*) And once I get my head round that cooker it might even get healthy.

Police sirens can be heard in the background getting louder and louder. **Tony** *looks worried. The sirens mix with the boom-boom of the music exactly as before. We hear the screeching of car tyres.* **Tony** *moves over to the bench again. He takes off his shirt. The music and sirens fade out.* **Tony,** *in his vest, frantically starts doing press-ups and sit-ups and burpees.*

Got to be fit. Boom fuckin' Boom. Turn that fuckin' music off! I know what you're tryin' to do. Turn it off. Bastards! (**Tony** *starts to shadow box around the cell*) I used to work with a guy called Ronald The Vest, old guy, been around since the dinosaur. We called 'im The Vest 'cos he had this thing about wearin' a bullet proof vest. It never worked. Supposed to be bullet proof, stab

proof, fuckin' bomb proof. Huge thing, it was, like a
continental quilt. He looked like the Michelin man. He
was the most stabbed man I ever met. Honestly, I never
met a man that got stabbed more. He got it everywhere;
in the face, the arms, the fingers – one psycho cut the
top of his ear off with a steak knife at the local Indian.
He even got stabbed up the arse one night by a bird
with a pair of nail scissors. But he never once got
stabbed in the vest.

Stops shadow boxing. Sits down.

I've never killed anyone. I bit a guy's ear off once. I bit
it clean off and spat it out. It hit my mate Harry on the
leg. I put it on a key ring and carried it around with me
for a few days, showing it to people, dropping it in their
beer, stuff like that. It was just a crack. I used to throw it
to the girls at the club and say, 'Catch'. They'd catch it,
then scream. Every time someone said, 'Do you wanna
beer, Tony?' I'd pull it out and say, 'No, 's all right, I've
got one ear!' Everyone'd crack up.

She said I was sick in the head. What does she know? I
saw her the other day. Out on the town with her mates.
Hen night or summat. Lost all her weight, got her
figure right back. Had this little dress on, dead short,

only just covered her internal organs. She looked nice.
Like she did the first night I met her all them years ago.
Brought back memories. I spoke. It was like talking to
an answering machine. Felt weird. Lot of blokes tryin'
to get in her pants. I held her hand. 'Maybe we could
talk,' I said. 'Yeah, maybe,' she said, but she didn't mean
it 'cos her words didn't reach her fingers. They just
died in my grip. There was no congruence, see. Words,
that's all, words with no attachment to emotion or
consequence. Then she went off with her mates. It
wasn't nice watching her leave. Without me. Imaginin' her
bein' porked by some other bloke, suckin' on some other.

I thought I killed a guy once, kicked him all round the
pub car park until me feet was sore. Me mates pulled us
off and tried to bring 'im round, but he wasn't having
any of it. Someone called an ambulance. All I could
hear was, 'He's dead, he's dead.' I thought I'd lost it. I
went home to her. She was in the pit when I got back. I
remember looking at her asleep in bed. I couldn't catch
my breath, she was so beautiful, like a princess. I
touched her skin. It was silk. I loved 'er in that moment
like I'd never loved another person. So beautiful. I
prayed to God, promised him that if he gave me one
more chance I'd change. Yeah, right. Lasted 'til the next
day when I heard he was all right.

Doorman

(Shakes his head and pats his ears as though trying to get the noise out)

Boom Boom fuckin' Boom. *(Pats ears)* They won't get me. I know what they're doin'. Turn it up as loud as you want! I can deal with this all day long. I fuckin' love it. Let's have some. I can handle it. I can handle it. 'S funny y' know, they're not like... I just never seen them as people, y' know, when I whacked 'em. You just do it. Harder the better. If you can spark 'em in one it's a bonus. When they're down you kick 'em 'til they stop moving... Then sometimes, most times, you kick 'em a bit more. Y' don't see them as people after a while. You don't think you're kicking someone's son, someone's husband. You don't think they've got kids. Y' never think they've got kids. Y' just can't think like that. You just 'ave t' do it, you 'ave to, 'cos if you don't the fuckers do it to you. It's your head bein' kicked around the pavement like a Coke can, it's your missus in the mourner's veil, it's your mother who gets the bad news before breakfast. You 'ave to, you... Listen, I've seen two of my mates on the cold slab from workin' this bastard trade, this thankless fuckin' bastard trade. One 'ad is throat cut by a slashing psycho with a craft knife, the other got his head stamped into a purée by a coachload of United fans on an away match.

Doorman

Beat

Apparently your man there went home right as ninepence. Bit of an 'eadache, felt a bit sick, tha's all. Went to bed... Never woke up again. Massive brain haemorrhage. Now 'e's dead. Dead. And I did it. I topped 'im. Boom Boom fuckin' Boom! Can we have the music a bit louder, please? Bit heavier on the base? Someone in fuckin' Florida reckons they can't fuckin' hear the fuckin' fuckin' thing. Fuckin' wankers. 'E arrested me. Lard Arse. Wasn't even his call. He just wanted to see my face. 'Ow does it feel knowing that you're not gonna see your kids for twelve years? ''Ow does it feel? Come on tell me, 'ow does it feel?' He just kept saying it over and over and fuckin' over.

All I could think of was me kids. Who's gonna tell them? How they gonna manage? I want to tell them. I can explain it, I don't want them talking to my fuckin' kids. Lard Arse just smiled and smiled and smiled. It was like it was painted on his fat face. Then 'e starts to laugh, a proper belly laugh, one of those you can't stop. And all I could think about was me and my kids. I thought about 'er too. I can 'andle it, I can 'andle it, I can 'andle it. Tiles on the floor. How many across? Eight. How many in length? Thirteen. How many in

60

total? 104, 104. How many tiles broken? How many fucking tiles are broken? How-many-tiles-are-fucking-broken?

Press-ups. (*Does some*) Sit-ups. (*Does some*) Burpees. (*Does some*) I didn't mean to kill him. I never meant to kill 'im. BOOM fuckin' BOOM! I wanna speak to my kids. I'm entitled to a phone call. You listening, you fat wanker, you fat fucking bastard? You hear me? You fuckin' hear me? Where's my phone call? I can 'andle it, I can 'andle it, I can 'andle it.

BLACKOUT

For full details of books and videos
by Geoff Thompson, visit:

www.geoffthompson.com